First World War
and Army of Occupation
War Diary
France, Belgium and Germany

GUARDS DIVISION
4 Guards Brigade
Coldstream Guards
3 Battalion
1 February 1918 - 31 October 1918

WO95/1226/1

The Naval & Military Press Ltd
www.nmarchive.com
Published in association with The National Archives

Published by

The Naval & Military Press Ltd

Unit 10 Ridgewood Industrial Park,

Uckfield, East Sussex,

TN22 5QE England

Tel: +44 (0) 1825 749494

www.naval-military-press.com

www.nmarchive.com

This diary has been reprinted in facsimile from the original. Any imperfections are inevitably reproduced and the quality may fall short of modern type and cartographic standards.

© **Crown Copyright**
Images reproduced by permission of The National Archives, London, England, 2015.

Contents

Document type	Place/Title	Date From	Date To
Heading	WO95/1226/1 4 Guards Brigade 3rd Bttn Coldstream Guards War Diary Feb-Oct 1918		
Heading	31st Division 4th Gds Bde 4th Bn Gren Gds Feb-Oct 1918 Diaries For Dates With 3 Guards Bde.		
Heading	31st Division 4th Gds Bde 3rd Bn Coldstream Gds. Feb-Oct 1918. attached 31 Div.		
Heading	War Diary. 3rd Battalion, Coldstream Guards. Vol. II, 1918. Period: From Feb. 1st, 1918. To Feb. 28th, 1918.		
War Diary	Arras	01/02/1918	08/02/1918
War Diary	Ecurie Wood	08/02/1918	21/02/1918
War Diary	Bailleul Willerval Line	21/02/1918	25/02/1918
War Diary	Trenches.	25/02/1918	28/02/1918
Heading	31st Division. 4th Guards Brigade. 3rd Battalion Coldstream Guards March 1918.		
Heading	War Diary of 3rd Bn. Coldstream Guards Volume III.- (1918.) Period:- March 1st To 31st 1918.		
War Diary	Trenches	01/03/1918	01/03/1918
War Diary	Bray. Camp.	02/03/1918	02/03/1918
War Diary	Tincques	03/03/1918	31/03/1918
Heading	4th Guards Brigade. 31st Division. 3rd Battalion Coldstream Guards April 1918.		
War Diary	Bienvillers	01/04/1918	01/04/1918
War Diary	Harluzel-Tincques	02/04/1918	02/04/1918
War Diary	Tincques.	03/04/1918	10/04/1918
War Diary	Tincques-Le Paradis	11/04/1918	11/04/1918
War Diary	Trenches	12/04/1918	13/04/1918
War Diary	Borre	14/04/1918	17/04/1918
War Diary	Le Tir Anglais	17/04/1918	23/04/1918
War Diary	Trenches	24/04/1918	27/04/1918
War Diary	Nr Hondeghem	28/04/1918	30/04/1918
Miscellaneous	A Form. Messages And Signals.		
Miscellaneous	Call Signs.		
Miscellaneous	From O.C. 6 N.F.	11/04/1918	11/04/1918
Miscellaneous	C.O. 3 C.G. R.5.	12/04/1918	12/04/1918
Miscellaneous	The Brigade Has Seen It And Wishes It Sent On To You. (sd) H.R. Alexander, Lt. Col. Comdg. 2nd Bn. Irish Guards.		
Miscellaneous	To O.C. 3 Coy.		
Miscellaneous	Regarding No. 1 Coy.		
Miscellaneous	To C.O. 3 C.G. V.1. 12th. Am Holding On And enfilading Enemy AAA From O.C. No. 3 Coy. 4.25. (Sd) V.N. Rowsell, Lt. O.C. No.3.		
Miscellaneous	O.C. 3 Coldstream.		
Miscellaneous	To Battns. T.M.B. 210 Fd. Coy. R.E. 95 F. Amblce. 12 K.O.Y.L.I. B.M.S. 213.	17/04/1918	17/04/1918
War Diary	Hondeghem	01/05/1918	20/05/1918
War Diary	Thievres	21/05/1918	31/05/1918
Heading	Guards Division 4th Gds Bde. 3rd-Bn. Colds. Gds June-Oct. 1918		
War Diary		01/06/1918	30/06/1918

War Diary		15/06/1918	15/06/1918
War Diary		10/06/1918	25/06/1918
Heading	War Diary of 3rd Bn. Coldstream Guards. Vol. VII, 1918. From 1st July, 1918 To 31st July, 1918.		
War Diary	La Cauchie	01/07/1918	31/07/1918
Heading	War Diary. 3rd. B.N. Coldstream Guards. Volume VIII. (1918) Period:- August 1st. To 31st. 1918.		
War Diary	Criel Plage	01/08/1918	31/08/1918
Heading	War Diary of 3rd Bn. Coldstream Guards. Vol. IX, 1918. Period : From 1st Sept. 1918, To 30th Sept. 1918.		
War Diary	Criel Plage	01/09/1918	23/09/1918
War Diary	Criel Plage.	17/09/1918	29/09/1918
War Diary	Criel Plage.	24/09/1918	30/09/1918
Miscellaneous	D.A.G., 3rd Echelon.	17/11/1918	17/11/1918
War Diary	Bray	01/10/1918	03/10/1918
War Diary	Frise	04/10/1918	11/10/1918
War Diary	Gouy	12/10/1918	15/10/1918
War Diary	Combles	16/10/1918	25/10/1918
War Diary	Criel Plage	26/10/1918	31/10/1918

WO 95
1226/1
3rd Bttn Coldstream Guards
War Diary
Feb - Oct 1918

4 Guards Brigade

31ST DIVISION.
4TH GDS BDE.

4TH BN GREN GDS.
FEB - ~~MAY~~ 1918

DIARIES FOR DATES
WITH 3 GUARDS BDE

Attached 31 DN

31ST DIVISION
4TH GDS BDE

3RD BN COLDSTREAM GDS.
FEB - OCT 1918

Attached 31 DIV

CONFIDENTIAL.

WAR DIARY.

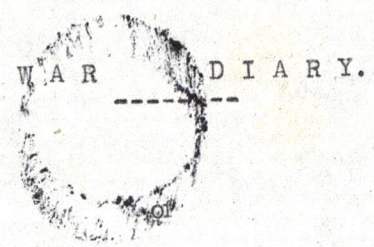

3rd Battalion, Coldstream Guards.

Vol. II, 1918.

Period :
From Feb. 1st, 1918.
To   Feb. 28th, 1918.

WAR DIARY
or
INTELLIGENCE SUMMARY.

(Erase heading not required.)

Army Form C. 2118.

Place	Date	Hour	Summary of Events and Information	Remarks and references to Appendices
ARRAS	1-2-18		In billets ECOLE Communale	
	2-2-18		Moved to billets in Rue D'AMIENS	
	3rd to 8th		Remained in their billets. The Bn found working large fatigues parties daily in the forward area	
ARRAS	8th		The Bn left the Rue d'Amiens and marched to EBURIE WOOD Camp arriving at 3.15 pm	
EBURIE WOOD	9th to 17th		An 11 company formation was adopted. BRIGADE the Bn did normal and platoon parades and specialist training as carried on during the period	
BAILLEUL MILLEKRUISE LYS	21st		The Bn relieved 2nd Bn Irish Guards in BAILLEUL–MILLEKRUISE Line B16 M 55 — B4 A 6 0 9	
	21st to 23rd		Remained in this line. Army [illeg] Grenade & OR. 10 Guard	
TRENCHES	28th		Relieved 2 Bn Irish Guards held Cam ARIEUX SECTOR B 12 M 87 to 7.30 a.m. – E. Z Rieux on an U.R.	
Trenches	25th 28th		Very quiet no casualties	

31st Division.
4th Guards Brigade.

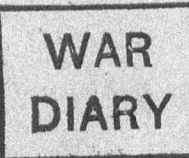

3rd BATTALION

COLDSTREAM GUARDS

MARCH 1918

<u>Confidential.</u>

— <u>WAR DIARY</u> —
of
<u>3rd Bn. Coldstream Guards</u>

— <u>Volume III</u> —
(1918.)

<u>Period</u>:— <u>March 1st to 31st 1918.</u>

WAR DIARY or INTELLIGENCE SUMMARY

Army Form C. 2118

Place	Date	Hour	Summary of Events and Information	Remarks and references to Appendices
TRENCHES	1.3.18		10 a.m. relieved. entrain at DAYLIGHT. RLY HEAD return to BRAY CAMP. arriving 8 p.m.	
BRAY.CAMP.	2.3.18		1 p.m. entrain arrive TINCQUES. 5 p.m.	
TINCQUES	3rd to 21st		Good billets. Company Training & Musketry. Inter Football Cup, & Bn Sports.	
	22nd		Emb. 10 a.m. detrain nr. BLAIREVILLE 7.30 p.m. elaining move up to ARMY 1st line	
	23rd		Remain in same position. 8 p.m. move forward and dig in in support on road slope hill between ERVILLERS and ST LEGER. In touch with 40.R.Div on our Right. Casualties 3.O.R. k in A.	
	24		Enemy retreated on our right from direction of MORY. 2 Coys form defensive flank with our Right on ERVILLERS. Casualties 20.O.R. 13 W.	
	25th & 26th		Heavy shelling. Enemy attack on our right. N/U. 8 a.m. withdrawal ordered Battalion T.O.A. 4.K. 3 W. 2 W.T. missing & missing Coys withdrawn & retired to withdraw dig in in their S.W of COURCELLES. 5 am ordered to withdraw to high ground S.W of AYETTE. 2 Coys E. of AYETTE - BUCQUOY RD. 8 p.m. 3 Coys withdrawn dig in S.E of DOUCHY - COMMIECOURT RD. O.R. 3 W. in A.	
	27th		In afternoon enemy driven back from heights COURCELLES. Quiet day. Casualties. O.R. 11 wounded & missing.	
	28.		1 am advance thro' line of AYETTE BUCQUOY RD. B2 w dis on own N/U. 2nd Lt 16 on own left. Heavy shelling, ordered to dig in & bombarded 7 am. 10 a.m. enemy attack on our right hop. not easily repulsed. Casualties Capt Fergus, & Kn A. to our night enemy pointed captive & AYETTE on our right. Cpl. Ledbetter & 12 others W in A. no further action. O.R. 6 k. 28 w. 7 miss. & 2 wounded Capt in A.	
	29-30		Quiet N/U. 31/1/1W received by 15 Lancs. relieve to RIENVILLERS. 5 wounded Casualties O.P. 3 k. Cot. F. Fitzgerald H. Col 3rd Bn Coldstream Guards	

TRENCHES

4th Guards Brigade.
31st Division.

3rd BATTALION

COLDSTREAM GUARDS

APRIL 1918.

WAR DIARY
or
INTELLIGENCE SUMMARY.

Army Form C. 2118.

3 Christian Ebo
Vol 31

Place	Date	Hour	Summary of Events and Information	Remarks and references to Appendices
BIENVILLERS	1.4.18		Raided Billets 2.0 a.m. from Couturelle 1.D.R. Went during relief 3.0 p.m. marched to Billets at WARLUZEL.	
WARLUZEL – TINCQUES	2.4.18 3.4 a. 9.4.18		Bn. entrained at noon & arrived TINCQUES 5.0 p.m. Batn. disembarked & training commenced.	
TINCQUES	10.4.18		5.0 · 6.30a Division inspected H.G. Guards Bn. pole in ceremonial — 11.0 a.m. march to ESTREE WAMIN of TINCQUES. Night was spent in saddleable units for lectures	
TINCQUES – LE PARADIS	11.4.18		11.0 a.m. busses arrived Brigade entrained & proceeded to STRAZEELE. Battn. marched to LE PARADIS where Bn. was billeted. Remainder of Brigade were billeted at VIEUX BERQUIN, RUE DE BOIS — LE ESTAIRES & OUTTERSTEENE Rd.	
	12.4.18		2.30 A.M. Battalion moved forward + took up position on Ridge near L'EPINETTE — in sectors ST. VENANT — LE CORNET PERDU. Had orders to hold this to Rifle a Bois Sud until 3rd K Div from of Rde at 5.0 a.m. on our front as opposite expected. Situation looked hair at dawn Dispositions as follows:— Front. 3 coy. echelon, 4 coy. Left coy. in extend S.E of ARRIWAGE. Rt. centre + rear coys by bombs held in front. 5.10 A.M. enemy reported advancing all along our front but were wiped out by machine gun fire. Kept away heavy machine gun fire SOMDRE Div held WILD BOAVRE RIVER. 11-0 A.M. No. 1 Coy. attacked & cone in College with No. 3 + 4 Coys nearly in advance. Heavy opposition with unlimited ammo of his rifles FMG from houses in LES PRESSEGEOUS Outposts S.W. of VIERHOECK. Patrol to support casualties who advanced on Sox. Div. front on No.1 Coys right flank disappeared (were not seen again) Wild reinforced all 3-0 p.m. were outflanked & shortly after casualties increasing Rt. 3-30 p.m. Sgt SAUBA went over & talked centre, S.W. of ARRIWAGE. 4 Coy also in direction of PONT TOURNANT — unable S.W. of ARRIWAGE. At this moment at about 4.20 p.m. 4 Cos. of No 1 Coy enemy troops attacked & assisted.Batn. being relieved by bombs of Sox. Div. enemy ran counter-attack. Cdn. held on until night fall — wd. 2nd unit & held frontier at PONT BEAULIEU Guard signal Rations & communication walked troops 9.	
	13.4.18		DODD & 7th Batns. were bombed at July 2hrs. Enemy assumed attack developed in Sector. Fight Back — and Cde. Bought to relief. Dispositions left of Sx. Div. troops our left by 1st Shrewds. at 6 x 10 p.m. Ridge M.G. lines in front off. Battn. Sox. & Cde. Boys — Remd. passed LEPINETTE FM to our left with outflanks in Coys from 1 a.m. casualties. 3 a.m. two enemy left by coys 3 O.M.L.I. & 5 S.E. of ARRIWAGE whilst No. 1 Coy (30 men all had reached by 2d a.m. M.G. 3 Coys C.M. to fight bay way back they were accounted by one Ridge field to the road. This attack towards our hardly defeated — 2 O.S of Ridge front dealt to attack about 5.0 A.M. was fairly attacked & coming off of our commenced & off prevented. forced to retire & retired a right guard to M.G. 4 were to the extreme new outflanked and off O.L.C. Manuel by M.G. but to man flanks and left of HIGH BEAULEU — ARRIWAGE Rd. Cde. ordered Batn. (about 4.0 m.) Celebrated 51st of — South S.E of ARRIWAGE. Guard might command to hold on and fight towards to bout	

Army Form C. 2118.

WAR DIARY
or
INTELLIGENCE SUMMARY.

(Erase heading not required.)

Instructions regarding War Diaries and Intelligence Summaries are contained in F. S. Regs., Part II. and the Staff Manual respectively. Title pages will be prepared in manuscript.

Place	Date	Hour	Summary of Events and Information	Remarks and references to Appendices
TRENCHES	13-4-18		Casualties for day:- Missing Capt Whitchurch, Lt Eveall, Capt Blome, Lieut Berry 2/Lt Mulliner 2/Lt Bethell W. O'Brien K in A 17 Ok R's M 259.	
BARRE	14-4-18		Bn marched to Barre HQ mess remainder under command A O.C. had Bks until casualties for 14-4. O.R. Kld 1, Wd 11, Missing 1.	
"	15/16/17-4-18		Battalion remained near BOIS — reorganised into 2 Coys	
LE TR ANGLAIS	18-4-18 to 20-4-18		Marched & took over trenches of O.B. & G.G. moved to BUSQUIMRON, LE TR ANGLAIS on 17th — two remained new dispositions.	
"	22-4-18 23-4-18 24-4-18		Battalion reorganised LA TR ANGLAIS Casualties 5 O.R. Wd Stats nil	
TRENCHES	2nd & 25-4-18 26-4-18		Quiet - relieved 3rd Irish Guards in front line & in BOIS D'AVAL, L.61, L.61 m Rgt, N Eng & Kew. left front line quiet with exception of very heavy gas shelling on night of 25/4/18 rel Casualties O.R. nil	
"	27-4-18		Relieved by 2nd Bn Royal Fusiliers returned to Billets near HONDEGHEM. Casualties O.R. Kld 1, Wd 32 (Gas)	
HONDEGHEM	28 — 30-4-18		Battalion in billets near HONDEGHEM. Find Coys drill of hundred	

Signed [illegible]
Lieut Col
Commanding
3rd Battalion Coldstream Guards

"A" Form
MESSAGES AND SIGNALS.

Prefix....Code.....m	Words.	Charge.	This message is on a/c of:	Recd. at.....m
Office of Origin and Service Instructions	Sent		.....Service.	Date.........
	At.........m			From.........
	To.........			
	By.........	(Signature of "Franking Officer.")	By.........

TO:
1. No 1 Coy 4th [illegible]
2. —
3. Quartermaster
4. Transport Officer

Sender's Number.	Day of Month.	In reply to Number.	
S.D. 1	10		AAA

1. The Battalion will move to MERVILLE area to-night 10/11 April.

2. (a) The Battalion will march to the ENBUSSING POINT

(b) Starting point. Rd. Junction ⅔ mile N.W. of the Church in VIEUX BERQUIN.

(c) Coys will be formed up with the heads of No 4 Coy at the starting point at 10.25 p.m.

(d) Order of March. B.H.Q, 4, 2, 1, 3.

(e) Dress. S.D. M.O with steel helmets & respirators. (Greatcoats will be worn.) Each man will carry 1 blanket rolled in the waterproof sheet. Capes will be carried. Each man will carry 2 grenades and 1 bandolier.

From		
Place		
Time		(continued)

The above may be forwarded as now corrected. (Z)

Censor. Signature of Addressee or person authorised to telegraph in his name.

* This line should be erased if not required.

"A" Form
MESSAGES AND SIGNALS.

Prefix......Code......m.	Words.	Charge.	This message is on a/c of:		Recd. at......m.
Office of Origin and Service Instructions	Sent				Date......
	At......m.		......Service.		From......
	To......				
	By......		(Signature of "Franking Officer.")		By......

TO — (2)

Sender's Number.	Day of Month.	In reply to Number.	AAA
S.D.1	10		

[handwritten message, largely illegible:]

1. [illegible] will at [illegible] Transport officer.
2. No [illegible] will be [illegible] the [illegible] for dump[?] of [illegible] will be [illegible] the quartermaster.
3. [illegible] for the move of the transport [illegible]
4. The transport will N.T. [illegible] the [illegible] battn under [illegible]
5. 5 [illegible] per [illegible] cook[?] [illegible] for B.H.Q will be carried on the [illegible].
6. Billeting Parties will travel in the leading [illegible] of the column. Report to the adjutant at the [illegible] on [illegible]

From ......
Place ......
Time ......

The above may be forwarded as now corrected. (Z)

......Censor. Signature of Addressor or person authorised to telegraph in his name.
This line should be erased if not required.

"A" Form
MESSAGES AND SIGNALS.

Prefix...Code...m,	Words.	Charge.	This message is on a/c of:	Recd. at:...m.
Office of Origin and Service Instructions	Sent		...Service.	Date...
	At...m.			From...
	To...			
	By...		(Signature of "Franking Officer.")	By...

TO—	3		

*Sender's Number.	Day of Month.	In reply to Number.	AAA
S.D.1	10		

6 Coys will be told off into
groups of 25.   one group of 25
to each 50 yards of road place.

7a. The EMBARKING POINT is from
100 yards W. of crossroads ½ mile S.W.
of front T of TINQUETTE and
eastward.

b) The Bnts will debris between VIEUX
BERQUIN and NEUF BERQUIN

8 Lewis guns and 2 magazines per gun
will be carried by the men. 2 Lewis
guns with 8 magazines per gun will be
attached to B.H.Q.

From		
Place		
Time		Conf.

The above may be forwarded as now corrected.   (Z)

Censor.   Signature of Addressor or person authorised to telegraph in his name.
* This line should be erased if not required.

"A" Form
MESSAGES AND SIGNALS.

Army Form C. 2121
(In pads of 100)

| Prefix...... Code...... m. | Words. | Charge. | This message is on a/c of: | Recd. at......m. |
| Office of Origin and Service Instructions | Sent At......m. To...... By...... | | ......Service. (Signature of "Franking Officer.") | Date...... From...... By...... |

TO { (4)

| Sender's Number. | Day of Month. | In reply to Number. | |
| S.3.1 | 18 | | AAA |

2.

Batta Hdrs will close at Villers
Brûlin at 10 pm and open
in the new area on completion
of the move.

My Map 1/A2.E (sheet 5A)
         LENS 11

From ......
Place ......
Time 7.15 pm

The above may be forwarded as now corrected. (Z) ......
Censor. Signature of Addressor or person authorised to telegraph in his name.
* This line should be erased if not required.

CALL SIGNS.

ADB.   4th Bn. Grenadier Guards.

ADX.   3rd Bn. Coldstream Guards.

ADF.   2nd Bn. Irish Guards.

ADI.   M.G. Coy ?

ADZ.   Brigade Headquarters.

From O.C. 6 N.F.   11.4.18.

I am holding on alright round VIERHOUCK with about 50 to 60 men. Could hold them up with help. Troops all round have retired.

9.37.a.m.   (sd) E. Temperley, Maj.

To ADB. ADX. ADF. ADI.
S.G. 558.   11.

On arrival at STRAZEELE about 8.30.p.m. Brigadier will see all C.Os at the head of the column AAA all concerned.
                              (sd) F.D. Mackenzie. Capt.
                                   Staff Capt. 4 Gds Bde.

To Commanding Officer, 3rd Bn. Coldstream Guards.
From E.W. Evans, Lt. No. 2 Coy. Place ARREWAGE. Time 11.30.p.m.

I am digging three posts each containing 10 men. I am in touch with Sgt. Vicars on my left and with Irish Guards No. 1 Coy on my right. I am told that a German Armoured Car patrols this road and throw out as a suggestion that a party of Sappers be detailed to blow up the road at a place about 100 yards from our line. Our Artillery dealing with this A. Car would be almost obliged to cause us casualties.
                              (sd) E.W. Evans, Lt.
P.S. Be careful if you ever cross this road to our posts as a sniper is doing good work here.

To A.D.X.   12th.
BMS.166.

Battalions will send down an officer to advanced brigade H.Q. VIEUX BERQUIN tomorrow morning to act as liaison officer AAA These officers must be well acquainted with the situation and country by daylight AAA Acknowledge.
From 4th Guards Brigade.
     1.20.a.m.   (sd) O. Lyttelton, Capt.

To:- 3 battalions 31 Div.
BMS.169.   12th.

4th Gds Bde will take up preliminary line road junction K.10.d.22 - N.E. along road to K.11.B.4.7 - thence LE CORNET PERDU - cross roads K.6.B.50.85 AAA 3 C.G. on right 4 G.G. on left 2 I.G. in reserve in E.29 central AAA Line of outposts will be established if possible South and East of PLATE BECQUE along line road junction K.16.d.5.2 - VIERHOUCK - road junction L.7.A.2.8. AAA Inter battalion boundary on outpost line road junction K.11.D.8.8 inclusive to 4 G.G. AAA Inter battalion boundary on main line road junction K.11.B.4.7 inclusive to 4 G.G. AAA Patrols will be pushed out to gain touch forward and on flanks AAA 50th Div reported to have posts at K.16 D.5.1. K.17 K.18 and 29th Div at L.7.A.2.7 AAA Advanced Brigade report centre school just W. of church VIEUX BERQUIN AAA Acknowledge.
From 4th Guards Brigade.
     4.30.a.m.   (sd) O. Lyttelton, Capt.

O.C. 3 C.G.   12.4.18.

Your L.2. received. I will advise further after attacking M.G. and seizing Bridge if possible.
By runner.   (sd) V.N. Rowsell, Lt.
     3.40.   O.C. No. 3 Coy.

C.O. 3 C.G.
R.5.   12.4.18.

At 4.30. after about 1½ sub barrage enemy advanced on our front but he failed to make any ground as we inflicted heavy casualties. Our casualties Nil. I should like the R.A. to get on to House with M.G. located in roof at K.16.B.33. It has 2 chimneys. Could do with some S.A.A. 20 Bandoliers to keep me going.
                            (sd) V.N. Rowsell, Lt.
    4.30.   O.C. No. 3 Coy.

17.

Receive message. People retiring on our right 6.15.a.m.
                            (sd) G.Barker, Sgt.
From Mr. Evans. 6.20. Enemy advancing on left and right. Right flank retiring.
                            (sd) G.Barker, Sgt.

To 3 Battalions - M.G. Coy.
BMS.173.   12th.

As soon as line K.16.d.6.2 - VIERHOUCK - cross roads L.7.A.2.7 has been gained it will become the main line of resistance and will be consolidated in depth. AAA Report dispositions as soon as possible AAA Acknowledge.
50th Div have troops in front so no difficulty should be met in gaining above line.
From 4th Gds Bde.
    7.10.a.m.   (sd) O. Lyttelton, Capt.

R.2.
O.C. 3 C.G.   12.4.18.

Enemy advancing on my front. Am quite prepared to deal with him
                            (sd) V.N. Rowsell, Lt.
    8.45.   O.C. No. 3 Coy.

To Adjt. 3 C.G. 12.4.18.

Germans advancing can be seen in large numbers at K.17.a & b. and 16.b. Artillery support please. Abrahams has just returned to say that it was impossible to get outposts to this point by day but has posted L.G. section and rifle section at K.16.b.7.3. Artillery support please. Am engaging them with rifle and L.G. fire.
From O.C. No. 4 Coy.
    8.55.a.m.   (sd) R.P. Elwes, Capt.

R.2.
To O.C. 3 C.G. 12.4.18.

Enemy brought up M.Gs or Tr.Mortars on 2 mules to K.18.d.9.9. We seem to have dealt effectively with these. Enemy infantry now shows strongly at K.17 a.5.8 to K.17.b.20.99. He also appears to be shooting from K.16.b. but I cannot locate him. I am in my front line at about K.11.c.cent. and it is extremely difficult and dangerous to send back messages. Enemy now appears to be making progress on my left and appears to be entering VIERHOUCK in considerable numbers. My position here is becoming precarious. No news from No. 2 Coy but they cannot any longer be effective in their old position. I can deal with my front. Enemy is now using light T.M. against me
                            (sd) R.P. Elwes, Capt.
T.M. is shooting from K.18.d I think. Enemy has now brought up guns and to same ref.
From O.C. No. 4 Coy.
    10.40.a.m.

O.C. 4 Grenadier Guards.
O.C. 3 Coldstream Guards.
I have received the following message from O.C. 6th N.F.
                                                The/

The Brigadier has seen it and wishes it sent on to you.
(sd) H.R. Alexander, Lt.Col.
10.15.a.m.   Comdg. 2nd Bn. Irish Guards.

O.C. 3 C.G.   12th.
Your 192 of 12th inst acknowledged and noted. No. 7 platoon will guard bridge PONT TOURNANT.
(sd) E.W. Evans, Lt. O.C. No. 2 Coy.

No. 3 Coy. Casualty Slip.
6324. Pte. Sutherland, T. Accidently burned. 11.4.18.
(sd) V.N. Rowsell, Lt. O.C. No. 3 Coy.
12.4.18.   3 C.G.

R.3.
O.C. 3 C.G.   12.4.18.
Enemy T.M. and M.Guns located at K.16.b.4.5.AAA Please ask Artillery to shell them AAA Just received verbal message from O.C. No. 2 Coy to withdraw on locality of K.10.D.2.8. AAA I have refused to do so without reasons and your orders.
11.15.   (sd) V.N. Rowsell, Lt. O.C. No. 3 Coy.

Adjt. 3 C.G.   R.3. 12.4.18.
Your message only reached me at 11.15.a.m. owing to orderly being wounded - it is also very bloody and illegible but have now deciphered it at 11.35.a.m. No. 3 Coy do not appear to have moved according to reports from my right. Enemy now have field gun in action at K.17.b.1.8. Situation otherwise unchanged except enemy snipers and M.Gs slightly less active from K.17.a. Await further orders before taking any action. Enemy snipers again becoming active. Enemy also have guns about K.18.cent and 24 a. and more have been reported seen arriving here. Have had about 6 casualties in these 2 platoons, don't know how they have fared in support. I have warned Lane to be prepared to bring up 1 platoon to support my left flank if necessary.
12 noon.   (sd) R.P. Elwes, Capt. O.C. No. 4 Coy.

O.C. 3 Coldstream Guards.   Copy.

The enemy have a battery of field guns situated in row of cottages on the company front and are firing grape shot direct.
10.45.a.m. received 1.25.p.m. (sd) A. Bowers, C.S.M.

Capt. R.T. Foster, MC. 12.4.
Dear Micky,
I have just seen the note to O.C. No.1. Will you please let me know if there are any orders for me to push on. Is No. 4 going to move forward? I can hold the bridge at K.16. B.5.6. with half No. 12 Platoon if No. 4 are not advancing otherwise I require to know exactly my objective in conjunction with the other coys as I have not seen previous orders in this connection.
(sd) V.N. Rowsell.

To ADB.ADX.ADF. 31 Bn. M.G.Corps.
SC.565.   12th.
A Brigade of the 5th Division are coming in tonight along the LA MOTTE - MERVILLE Road AAA addsd all concerned rptd Bde Advd. Hdqrs.
From ADZ.   (sd) G. Furze, Capt.
for Staff Captain, 4th Gds Bde.

To ADZ.
L.1.   12th.
Attempted to advance K.16.b. but advance impossible by enemy M.G. covering bridge 16.b. central. No movement possible in front line owing to enemy M.G. and rifle fire from houses K.17.a & b AAA 1 Coy of 1st I.G. have moved up to cross rd K.10.d. AAA
From 3 C.G.
2.p.m.

To O.C. 3 Coy.

L.2.   12th.
An advance was ordered at 11.a.m. No. 1 Coy on right, 3 centre 4 left. AAA No. 1 report they attempted and failed AAA I conclude owing to M.G. fire covering Bridge K.16.b.5.5. If possible seize bridge to help future advance AAA General advance of 3 Coys will not take place until further orders AAA
From 3 C.G.
    2.45.p.m.   (sd) F. Longueville, Lt. Col.

To 4 G.G. 3 C.G. 2 I.G.   12th.

Brigade Headquarters close at VIEUX BERQUIN at 4.p.m. and reopen at LE PARADIS at same hour.
From 4 Gds Bde.   (sd) D.J. Knight, Lt. I.O.

To 4 G.G. 3 C.G.
BM 185.   12th.

149 and 87 brigades together are endeavouring to take up line with their right about K.6.b.5.9. and left about BLEU joining 92nd Brigade which continues line N.E. through HTE MAISON AAA Border Regiment is reported by 87 Brigade as on immediate left of Grenadiers AAA On right 151 Bde reports holding from U.16.c.00 Southwards through LE SART (U.27.c) AAA Try to take on Hun field guns with your lewis guns.
From 4 Gds Bde.
    2.45.p.m.   (sd) L.J.P. Butler. B.G.

To 4 G.G. 3 C.G.
BM.186.   12th.

Am informed by an officer just returned from there that Border Regt. with other details is holding line on your left rear from LA COURONNE to BLEU AAA Enemy about F.25.d. F.2.6.c.
From 4 Gds Bde.
    3.10.p.m.   (sd) L.J.P. Butler, B.G.

To O.C. 3 C.G. 12th.
Sir,
    The Lewis Gun is in position commanding the bridgehead. There are there Mr. Leadbitter, 1 Cpl and 3 men. These I am reinforcing as soon as possible. With this Lewis Gun team there are 1 Sgt and 6 men of the D.L.I. and on their left are about 25 men of the D.L.I. and Y. and Lancs. As soon as it gets dusk I am sending a composite platoon of 6, 7 and 8 to dig in on a line approx. parallel to the word TOURNANT and just NORTH of it. Mr. Merriman and Mr. Miller will be with this party and they will have 2 lewis guns. The officers have instructions to get in touch with No. 1. Coy and the D.L.I. I am not shifting the D.L.I. and Y. and Lancs yet till I can see how the situation is. No. 5 platoon will remain at the farm under Mr. Evans. I have seen the officer in charge of the company of I. Guards and he is sending up at dusk 2 platoons to dig in in support. They will be approx just SOUTH of the corner of the orchard which is due NORTH of the "T" in TOURNANT. Since the attack I have had no reply to your Note to No. 1. Ammunition, Lewis Gun hoppers and oil are wanted badly.

    3.25.p.m.   (sd) R.T. Foster, Capt.

Regarding No. 1 Coy.

Evans received a message from the S.M. of No. 1 Coy to the effect that they went forward this morning, but were met with heavy ~~fire,~~ rifle and machine gun fire, and after suffering heavy casualties retired to their original line where they are at present. The S.M. had not seen Mr Whitaker.

To O.C. 3 C.G.
Sir,
    The enemy attacked No. 1 Coy this afternoon about 3.45 and they fell back. I counter-attacked with the coy of I.G. and have got back some of the ground. I would have got it all but...........cannot walk. There are two officers left and practically no men, and we got back the original line. Must have some more men at once.
                                (sd) R.T. Foster.
Scene of attack K.16.a.

---

4 G.G., 3 C.G. 1 I.G.
BM.189.   12th.
A brigade of 5th Division is coming in tonight along LA MOTTE-MERVILLE road AAA Very important that you should let me know your dispositions especially on flanks of the brigade at dusk AAA Situation on left is not good AAA Enemy is in BUTTERSTENE AAA Our line runs approximately LA COURONNE - FME LABIS - MERRIS AAA Any withdrawal forced on us should be made so as to face the enemy Eastwards rather than S.E. as at present AAA VIEUX BERQUIN must be held.
From 4 Gds Bde.
3.45.p.m.   (sd) L.J.P. Butler, B.G.

BMS.189;   12th.
The line to be held tonight and tomorrow will be PT TOURNANT K.15.D - L'EPINETTE - LA COURONNE where it will join the 12th K.O.Y.L.I. who will carry the line northwards along the eastern outskirts of VIEUX BERQUIN towards MERISIS AAA At dusk the line will be organised on a three battalion front as follows Irish Guards from Pt TOURNANT to a line drawn from N.W. to S.E. through point K.10.d.5.6 AAA Coldstream thence to line drawn N.W. and S.E. through the house at K.5.D.8.6. AAA Grenadiers thence to join the right of K.O.Y.L.I. about 300 yards S. of LA COURONNE AAA O.C. Irish Guards must arrange with troops of 50th Division on right to withdraw his two companies now S. of the canal AAA It is hoped that 5th Division will take over line from PT. TOURNANT - L'EPINETTE in which case Irish Guards will form Brigade reserve selecting a position about K.4 facing E. and right flank facing S.E. AAA Coldstream company thus relieved will be in battalion reserve AAA 33rd Division is moving up from METEREN towards MERRIS and 1st Australian Division is beginning to arrive about STRAZEELE AAA 5th Division arriving on our right is also fresh AAA Brigade H.Q. will open LA RUE DU BOIS about K.21.A.7.4. forthwith AAA Acknowledge.
From 4th Guards Brigade.   (sd) O. Lyttelton, Capt.

To ADX.
S.C. 564.   12th.
Re copy of attached message. As same was received at 1.25.p.m. the running having missed his way no action has been taken beyond reporting same to D.H.Q. and advanced Bde Hd.Qrs.
From ADZ rear.   (sd) G.Furze. Captain,
                                      Staff Captain 4 Gds Bde.

To ADX.   12th.
Your A.198 received AAA. C.O. is now on your right flank seeing what can be done AAA A.D.B. ~~can-be-do~~ have formed defensive flank on their left AAA
From A.D.F.   (sd) Charles Moore,
                                                  I.G.

To C.O. 3 C.G.
V.1.   12th.
Am holding on and enfilading enemy AAA
From O.C. No. 3 Coy.   4.25.   (sd) V.N. Rowsell, Lt. O.C. No.3.

R.9.   13th.
To C.O. 3 C.G.
Attack developing on left flank. Enemy tank in action up and down K.16.D.
    6.55.a.m.   (sd) V.N. Rowsell, Lt. O.C. No.3.
Later. Situation quieter.

R.10.   13.4.18.
To Adjt. 3 C.G.
Two boxes Hales Grenades would be very useful. Can you let me have them today, also some Very lights, as none were drawn before coming up. I also require 40 more shovels as on the day we came up Major Gillilan only permitted one every third man for 2 platoons and one every other man for the remainder.
    7.15.a.m. by Pte.Tailly.   (sd) V.N. Rowsell, Lt. O.C.No.3.

R.11.   13.4.18.   Situation Report.
Enemy. Quiet night with no shelling on Coy Front.
Work.   Improved trenches and commenced communication trench
        between left front and support line.
Disposition. Unchanged.
    7.15.a.m. By runner.   (sd) V.N. Rowsell, Lt. O.C.No.3.
                                                                 Coy.

O.C. 3 C.G.   13.4.
No. 2 appear to be pressed on my right. They have about 8 men and some I.G. under Mr Evans at an advance post. The position is bad. No. 1 cannot be found. I await your orders. I have given them 1 Platoon and with 1 doing picquet have with me 2 weak ones.   (sd) V.N. Rowsell, Lt. O.C. No.3.
    1.30.p.m.   Coy.

From O.C. No. 1 Coy.
To   O.C. 3 C.G.
1. Situation normal. Enemy about 400 yds to right front. No
   signs of enemy attack.
2. Map reference not known. No map.
3. Coy attacked at 11.a.m. and advanced to 500 or 600 yds.
   Casualties extremely heavy, mainly through cross fire of
   snipers and M.Gs. Coy retired about 12 noon by platoons.
   Casualties again heavy causing complete disorganization.
4. Present strength about 40 all told. Ordered by 2nd Lt.
   Leadbitter to retire at 4.a.m. now in position with D.C.L.I.
   and 1 I.G.
    7.25.a.m.   (sd) E.R. Vickers, Sgt.

O.C. 3 C.G.   13.4.18.
I have not withdrawn from my position or commenced digging new line owing to heavy machine gun fire and the fog lifting. Please let me know if this right.
    9.20.a.m.   (sd) E.W. Evans, Lt.

From O.C. No. 4 Coy. 13.4.18.
To   O.C. 3 C.G.
Shortly before dawn owing to inability to gain touch with 4th G.G. on my left I moved 2 platoons to take up position ordered G.G. on my left by you. I myself took up my H.Q. with 14 platoon at K.11.b.15.80 this platoon holding K.11.b.0.5 to K.11.b.3.9. 2 sections of 15 platoon from K.5.d.35.0.5 to d.5.5. 16 platoon from 5.d.6.5 to 5.d.8.9. the remainder of my coy spreading out over my previous line from K.11.b.0.5 to 11 cent to 11.C.2.4. I left this half of the Coy under Mr Lane with orders to maintain touch with No. 3 Coy and obtain from them 1 platoon to strengthen his line if the expected relief did not materialise. Just before dawn I discovered a coy of G.G. dug in from about K.5.c.7.6 to about 5.b.9.2. Shortly after dawn the enemy under cover of a thick fog attacked my position but I was able to hold him. At

about 7.30.a.m. Sgt Toogood who was with Mr. Lane's
command arrived and reported that he and Mr. Lane had been
unable to find No. 3 Coy although he reported having found
their trench empty. Their position was then attacked and
this N.C.O. reports pierced on both flanks so that they were
forced to fall back onto the right of the Grenadier lines in
K.5.c. This withdrawal left my right exposed and L'EPINETTE
unguarded. I therefore ordered Sgt. Toogood (Mr. Lane failed
to reach Coy H.Q.) to form a defensive flank on my right and
send out a patrol to try and gain touch with troops on my
right. At 8.15.a.m. Sgt. Bright arrived and reported that
15 and 16 platoons had been attacked by Germans who called
themselves "King's Coy. Grenadiers" and forced to withdraw
to left of Grenadier line K.5.d. & b thus leaving my left
flank in the air. At 8.20.a.m. enemy succeeded in capturing
L'EPINETTE and enfilading my position so that I was forced to
fall back to Grenadier line K.5.c & d where I now am.
Troops appear to be digging in on my right about K.4.b. and I
have sent out a patrol to gain touch. Germans are now
making a heavy attack on LE CORNET PERDU but should not meet
with success. I shall hold this position until I receive
orders from you.
  9.30.a.m.   (sd) R.P. Elwes, Capt.
           O.C. No. 4 Coy.

To 4 G.G. 3 C.G. 2 I.G. 12 K.O.Y.L.I.
BM.194.   13th.
Our front line runs approximately Pt TOURNANT - K.10.d -
LA COURONNE - E.24.b. thence details of 29th Div. hold to Fme
LABIC AAA They are in good form and well dug in AAA thence 92
Bde line runs via Fme LYNDE - MERRIS. Behind us an Australian
Brigade is dug in thus - 1 battalion from K.14.d to E.28.c.
1 battalion from E.28.c. to E.17.a. 1 battalion from LA MOTTE
to E.15.a. 1 battalion about D.17.
From 4 Gds Bde.
  10.5.a.m.   (sd) L.J.P. Butler,B.G.

From O.C. No. 1 Coy. (Sgt Vickers).
To O.C. 3 C.G.
Sir,
  Owing to No. 4 Coy having to evacuate L'EPINETTE, I have
dug in in a line directly behind the farm of L'EPINETTE. Am
in touch with Cornwall L.I. on right and 4 Coy on left.
Extent of front 400 yds.
           (sd) E.R. Vickers, Sgt.

To D.L.I.
A.215.   13th.
Am forming defensive flank K.10.C.5.5. AAA 4th G.G. are
continuing this S.E. of GARS BRUGGHE.
From 3 C.G. 10.25.a.m.   (sd) P.A. Clutterbuck.

3.G.G.
Presume you mean D.C.L.I. This arrangement will do well.
As we are holding the line from K.15.b.1/9 - about K.11.b.
central. We have established a strong post at K.4.c.3/2.
In the event of our being overpowered we shall hold the line
ARREWAGE - MERVILLE road at all costs: this is an order from
our Brigade.   (sd) T.M. RAWLIN,Capt.Adjt.
11.40.a.m.   1 D.C.L.I.

4.G.G. 3 C.G. 2 I.G. 1 K.O.Y.L.I.
BM.195.   13th.
If compelled to retire Brigade will take up line S.E. corner
of BOIS DAVAL - VERTE RUE - LA COURONNE AAA Should this
be much enfiladed the senior C.O. must give the necessary
orders (but there must be no retirement without orders from
Bde H.Q.) to swing back left and hold line S.E. corner of
BOIS DAVAL - VIEUX BERQUIN Church to point of junction between
12 K.O.Y.L.I. and details of 29 Div about E.24.b.47.
Acknowledge by next runner or by wire.
From 4 Gds Bde. 10.30.a.m.   (sd) L.J.P. Butler, B.G.

O.C. 3 Coldstream.
From Lt.E.Evans.
Have collected a few Guards and am mixed up with D.C.L.I.
to help hold the line which they dug last night. Miller
and Rowsell's men passed through me so I brought my 10 men
away from post which was enfiladed.
                                            (sd) E.W. Evans.

Adjt. 3 C.Guards.   R.45.
The following explanation as given by O.C. our left coy.
(1). My left is at present 500 yds east of ARREWAGE - MERVILLE road.
(2). My line is in continuation of the coy on my right.
(3). 50 guards have made a defensive flank on my left.
(4). A platoon of the support coy has reported to me and they are continuing the line towards L'EPINETTE.
(5). I have sent an officer to find the Guards right.

From the above it appears that the Germans hold L'EPINETTE,
but that there is a continuous line including your defensive
flank. I am sending back two of your men who have got
detached from your battalion to our front line coy.
    2.20.p.m.   (sd) T.M. Rawlin, Capt.Adjt.
                                                  D.C.L.I.

Our Brigade have just ordered us to reinforce our left with
one company. This coy will reinforce our left and probably
overlap your defensive flank. Please let me know of any
special orders you wish given to this company and let me
know reference of your Battalion H.Qs. My runner will await
reply.
                                      (sd) T.M.R.

To C.O. Coldstream Guards.
Enemy advancing from LA COURONNE in direction of RUE DU BOIS.
I am in action and firing. About 100 seen. I am at /E.28.c.
3.7. (approx) with good field of fire for 1000 yds.
                                    (sd) G.M.B. Watkins, Lt.
                                    "C" Company 31st M.G. Battn.

To O.C. Coldstream and Grenadier.
Men seen retiring from VIEUX BERQUIN - COURONNE line, going
west - do not know the situation. German M.G. fire heavy.
                                    (sd) R.V. Bailey, Capt.
                              O.C."C" Company 31 M.G. Battn.
Digging in on west of road.

ADB.ADX.ADF.
SC.573.   13th.
Please give date and name of all officer casualties when
submitting your estimated casualty return (consolidated) this
afternoon AAA If many casualties occur during afternoon
another estimated casualty wire should be submitted tonight
AAA Addsd all concerned.
From ADZ.   (sd) E.D. Mackenzie, Capt.
                                    Staff Captain, 4 Gds Bde.

To ADX.
A.125.   15th.
Ref.my A.120 of today.AAA Follg.casualties to Officers ADX
AAA Wounded Capt.R.T.Foster MC., Lieut. C.E. Raphael, 2nd
Lt. E.C.B. Merriman, 2nd Lt. D.H. Scott AAA Wounded and
missing Lieut. V.N. Rowsell AAA Missing Captain R.P. Elwes,
Lieut. J.A.C. Whitaker, 2nd Lt. J.Ashby, 2nd Lt. W.A.Millar,
2nd Lt. A.C.L. Abrahams, 2nd Lt. A.M. Carr, 2nd Lt. C.O.
Leadbitter AAA ADX will wire dates as soon as possible AAA
Addsd Y.C.A. rptd ADX.
From ADZ.   (sd) G. Furze, Lt.

To Battns. T.M.B. 210 Fd.Coy.R.E. 95 F.Amblce. 12K.O.Y.L.I.
B.M.S.213.   15/4
                                                    however
There is no change in the situation AAA The Brigade is at
one hour's notice to man the HAZEBROUCK defences AAA a
description of these defences giving sectors etc. will be
issued later AAA Acknowledge.
From 4th Guards Brigade.
                    (sd) O. Lyttelton.Capt.

4th Guards Brigade.

Herewith Casualties as verified up to date:-

Capt. R.T. Foster, Wounded 12.4.18.
2/Lt. E.C.B. Merriman, Wounded 12.4.18.
2/Lt. D.H. Scott, Wounded 12.4.18.
Lieut. J.A.C.Whitaker, Wounded - Missing 13.4.18.
Lieut. C.E. Raphael, Wounded 13.4.18.
2/Lt. A.M. Carr. Missing 13.4.18.
2/Lt. W.A. Millar, Missing 13.4.18.
2/Lt. C.O. Leadbitter, Missing 13.4.18.
2/Lt. J. Ashley, Missing 13.4.18.
2/Lt. A.C.L. Abrahams, Missing 13.4.18.
Capt. R.P. Elwes, Missing 13.4.18.
Lieut. V.N. Rowsell, Wounded - Missing, 13.4.18.

Other Ranks.

	K.	W.	M.	W.M.	
12th.	14	@61	10	3	= 88
13th.	15	73	260	24	= 372
14th.	1	11	1		= 13
	30	145	271	27	= 473

@ included 3 Wounded at duty.

17.4.18.

Army Form C. 2118.

WAR DIARY 3rd Battn
or
INTELLIGENCE SUMMARY. Coldstream Guards
(Erase heading not required.)

Vol. 41

May 1918

Place	Date	Hour	Summary of Events and Information	Remarks and references to Appendices
Hondeghem	May 1st - May 20th		Battn in billets and tents. Captured on 15/5/18 Return sent (I.O.R wounded 4/5/18)	
THIEVRES	May 21st - May 31st		Battn moved by bn train and made route To billets at THIEVRES. Battn training route marching and musketry daily	

R.V.S. Cranfurd
Lt Col.
Cmg 3rd Batt Coldstream Guards

Guards Division
4th Gds Bde
3rd Bn Colds: Gds
June – Oct 1918

3rd Battn Coldstream Gds

WAR DIARY
or
INTELLIGENCE SUMMARY
(Erase heading not required.)

JUNE 1915.

Army Form C. 2118.

Place	Date	Hour	Summary of Events and Information	Remarks and references to Appendices
	June 1st		at THIEVRES. Battn in the Grove area in Cafes. Two Coys Remainder	
Bray	6		in the Cafes and Two Coys in huts. Bn HQ Lodge Hty. 26 S H Q hrs	
Two Coys			marched early in Morning, to arrange concentrated by Brigadier	
	June 7th		Ranforcements Joined G H 3 Offrs & 242 R + F. Details unallotted at time	
			at THIEVRES G.H.Q. at 11.20 am	
	June 8 - 30		Whole Battn employed daily in digging trenches near THIEVRES & BRAS & MO	
	June 19		Arrival at HQ Major F. W. Prinked MC Rgt (from some) Commanding Coy	
			at Bn HQ	
			Lt Sassoons (Chas) & Lieut Jonty Ambrose Mc	
	21 May		2/Lt Man. B.E. van a board.	

A.5834. Wt. W4973/M687. 750,000 8/16 D.D. & L. Ltd. Forms/C.2118/13.

CONFIDENTIAL.

WAR DIARY

OF

3rd Bn. Coldstream Guards.

Vol. VII, 1918.

FROM: 1st July, 1918
TO : 31st July, 1918.

WAR DIARY or INTELLIGENCE SUMMARY

Army Form C. 2118.

3rd Batt: Coldstream Gds

Place	Date	Hour	Summary of Events and Information	Remarks and references to Appendices
LA BAUCHIE	July 1st	5.15	Batt: employed daily in making trenches. Fine Gun work daily.	
	July 9th		Batt: entrained at MONDICOURT. PAS arrived and left at 2.30 p.m. & proceeded by rail to EU ... (via Boulogne & Fauvilles) & then ... Tours at ... & marched to CRIEL PLAGE arriving in Camp ... (15°) Arrived early 9 July 9th.	
	July 10th & 28th		Batt: employed in constructing system of camps and preparing for the arrival of "Young Officers" who were sent to us after ... to ...	
	July 29th 30th		Draft of four officers, made up to ... in addition to some support Batt's received ... ... from outpost - signed July 29.	

Signed
Lt. Col.
Comd. 3rd Batt. Coldstream Gds

SECRET.

WAR DIARY.

3RD. BN. COLDSTREAM GUARDS.

VOLUME VIII.

(1918)

Period :-

AUGUST 1ST. to 31ST. 1918.

WAR DIARY
INTELLIGENCE SUMMARY

3rd Batt. Coldstream Gds

August 1917

Place	Date	Hour	Summary of Events and Information	Remarks and references to Appendices
CRIEL PLAGE	1st–25th		Battn. employed daily on training for open warfare & route marching.	
	26th		Instructor of one hundred attached non-commissioned officers continued by selected Instructors.	
	26th		A draft of 200 O.R. S/gt the Battalion to join Battalion in the line	
	27th		Young Officers course Commenced	
	28th		Young Officers left to join their Battalion.	
	31st		A draft of 8 Officers and 250 O.R. left to join the Battalion in the line.	

RH Law Jones Lt Col
Co. 3rd Batt Coldstream

CONFIDENTIAL.

WAR DIARY

OF

3rd Bn. Coldstream Guards.

Vol. IX, 1918.

PERIOD:

From 1st Sept. 1918,
To   30th Sept. 1918.

WAR DIARY
or
INTELLIGENCE SUMMARY

Army Form C. 2118.

3rd Batt. Coldstream Gds

September 1918

Place	Date	Hour	Summary of Events and Information	Remarks and references to Appendices
CRIEL PLAGE	16-23rd		Batt: worthy employed undergoing in Young Officer School. Suspection men formed into classes for instruction in Lewis Gun, Bomb, Rifle - Bon-bing - Map reading & Scouting.	
	17th		Draft of 1 Off. and 103 O.R. arrived from Base.	
	18th		" 2 " 73 " " "	
	29th		" 2 " 12 " " "	
	24th		Batt: marched to E.V. thence entrained to COMTEVILLE and marched to billets in DOMLEGER and AGENVILLE	
	27th		Batt: entrained at 7.30 p.m. and proceeded to CHUIGNOLLES arriving there at 3 a.m. (2 miles)	
	28th		Batt: moved by bus to BRAY (2 miles)	
	29-30th		Batt: in billets at BRAY at late stage to more to when Corps.	

M.M. [signature] Lt. Colonel
Comdg. 3rd Batt Coldm Gds.

1 OCT 1918
3rd BATTALION COLDSTREAM GUARDS

D. A. G.,
   3RD ECHELON.

Rejoined 1st Gds. Bde.
7/11/18

Herewith War Diary for the Battalion under my Command for the month of October, 1918, instructions having been received from 4th Guards Brigade to send you this direct, quoting their Officer letter of 3-11-18, 4 G.B. 4/38.

W.H.V. Crawfurd
            Lieut. Colonel,
            Commanding,
3RD BATTALION COLDSTREAM GUARDS.

Army Form C. 2118.

WAR DIARY or INTELLIGENCE SUMMARY.

(1) October 1915 3rd Battn. Coldstream Guards

(Erase heading not required.)

Vol 46

Place	Date	Hour	Summary of Events and Information	Remarks and references to Appendices
BRAY	1st	—	Battn. in billets.	
	2nd	—	Battn. entrained and moved in *two* columns to BRIE where returned to billets in BRAY in evening.	
	3rd	—	Battn's. own transport and personel [sic] to BRIE and returned in convoy to billets at FRISE	
FRISE	4-5	—	Battn. in billets and huts at FRISE. Drafts of 2 off. + 155 O.R. arrived	
	6th	—	Battn. left in lorries at 3.30 a.m. and marched in rear of Bgde. Halts for the night near BELLENGLISE. Batt. bivouacked in town as ordered	
	9th	—	Battn. moved up again in lorries to head the advance and Bttn. to night near TREMONT. Slight firing by rifles from Battn. transport in town.	
	10th	—	Battn. again moved up and billets for night near TOERTRY.	
	11th	—	Battn. returned to billets in attack of GOUY.	

A.5834   Wt.W4973/M687   750,000   8/16   D.D.&L.Ltd. Forms/C.2118/13.

WAR DIARY or INTELLIGENCE SUMMARY

Army Form C. 2118.

(2) Octr. 1918   3rd Battn. Coldstream Gds.

Place	Date	Hour	Summary of Events and Information	Remarks and references to Appendices
GOUY	12th	15th	Battn. in billets at GOUY.	
COMBLES	16th		Battn. moved by train to COMBLES and en-trained in tents and dug-outs.	
"	17th–24th		LEUZE WOOD in tents and dug-outs. Battn. employed finding fatigues in the way from 1 Offr. & Guards Div. Infantry to 1 Offr. & 65 O.R. found Battn. 22.10.18 Battn. entrained at BAPAUME and moved to E.V. Army then on day 26.10.18 when Battn. marched to station camps at CRIEL PLAGE.	
CRIEL PLAGE	26th–31st		Battn. emp. by al. Training and marching. Strength on 31st 16 Offrs. & 210 O.R. and in admin reinforcement Camp 1 Offr. & 85.	

[stamp: 3RD BATTALION COLDSTREAM GUARDS 1 NOV 1918]

M.H. Crawford Lt Col
Comdg. 3rd Battn. Coldstream Gds.

www.ingramcontent.com/pod-product-compliance
Lightning Source LLC
Chambersburg PA
CBHW081500160426
43193CB00013B/2547